First Printing 2013

First Edition

ISBN 978-0-9706103-1-7

 0-9706103-1-9

Published by Ancient Legacy Press

Cover art & Pictures by Jyade Cythrawl

<u>Other Books by Jyade Cythrawl</u>

The Legacy & The Secret Wisdom of the Black Arts

<u>Forth Coming</u>

Demonic Magic

True Black Magic & the Alchemy of Darkness

The Illustrated Underworld

If you wish to contact the author of this book,

Please email: Jyadec@aol.com

We enjoy hearing from you and appreciate your interest, however we cannot guarantee a response to every letter.

This book is dedicated to my sister Vivian

CONTENTS

ACKNOWLEDGMENTS

I WOULD LIKE TO THANK ALL OF MY READERS
AND THOSE WHO HAVE EMBARKED UPON THE
PATH OF DARKNESS & THE UNDERWORLD, IN
ONE WAY OF ANOTHER. I WOULD ALSO LIKE TO
THANK THE SPIRITS, AS NONE OF THIS WOULD
BE POSSIBLE WITHOUT THEM. THIS IS THEIR
STORY AS WELL AS MINE.

Preface

This tome tells the story of my tragedy; my journey through the void of madness, the Underworld and my eventual transformation and the wisdom I received from the Spirits; and by experience, trial, and tribulation. As I wrote these pages and reflected on my life, I never intended for its publication, however a story of the Underworld and its inhabitants it does indeed tell. It may well help others on the path to understand their trials, or get to know the trials, spirits, and experiences I went through more clearly. I have now decided to release it in the hopes that my dear readers will better understand me and my work, what I went through and how I came to be who I am today. However, this was only one part of my personal journey, the beginning, for it never stops. We're always living, learning, and going through something at some point in our lives.

My story is not an easy one to tell. It began long, long ago but the relationship mentioned initially in this book is what finally sent me over the edge, completely. No, it was not only a relationship that could cause such devastation, but also all that had transpired because of it, this was the catalyst and the will of the spirits. They eventually changed the course of my life, and I became someone completely different.

Originally this was only going to be a book of poetry, but I realized without all of the parts that I have decided to include, it would have never been able to relate the entire ordeal or the lessons learned by such tribulation. Therefore, I have written about the some of the stories that lead to the inspiration, in hopes that you may then be able to understand the full impact and pain that this poetry reveals.

Only if we fall can we be transformed.

Looking back on my adventure into the uncharted depths of hell I would probably do it all again. What's this? You say I'm mad. Maybe, but I can tell you this, it was the most interesting, devastating, agonizing, inter-dimensional, memorable adventure that anyone could ever undertake. Never a dull moment!

Darkness and the trip into the Underworld is a two edged sword. The first does not guarantee your survival, but if you do, you will not believe the things you will be shown and open to, and who you will become!

Jyade

Chapter One

In The beginning

This chapter will serve as an introduction into the actual relationship. Originally this was only going to be a book of poetry, but I realized without all of the parts that I have decided to include, it would have never been able to relate the entire ordeal or the lessons learned by such tribulation. Therefore, I am including this summary in hopes that you may then be able to understand the full impact and pain that this poetry reveals.

I can't change what I've become, but every now and then a little moral support from my family would be in order. But, considering the circumstances of my divorce one might see something to it. But that which lies at the surface is just that, the tip of the iceberg. No one ever looked any further into my life. They all saw how miserable I was, but chose to turn away. From their point of view the logic was this, if we pretend nothing is wrong, then nothing can change and life will keep its steady pace and we will not rock the boat.

Never ending torment from my husband is what my life consisted of. Day in and day out - for ten long years. But that chapter of my life is closed and behind me now, along with the rest of my dreams and fantasies of love. I walk on now, alone, through the mists of time like a ghost, an apparition of what I once was. All of my illusions have been taken, especially those of love. No, rather I have given them up, they no longer serve me any purpose, they only hinder me from truth.

What a shame that we can deceive ourselves with all of the frivolities and lies of our lives. Always being conditioned by someone or something on how to think and how to act, or what to feel. Are we then any better or worse off knowing what truth is? Probably not, it's got to be a personal choice. Some find comfort in being blissfully ignorant, or maybe they find comfort in reading the 'blue prints' to life. Regardless, truth is terrifying. It will rip you up and spit you back out. It has no mercy but it rewards one with wisdom. Truth is not for everyone, but I have been afforded the opportunity to go where most would not dare to tread. I have found truth. I have no soul or song in my heart now, but I have found some truth, and now I can never go back to the way I once was. My life now lays around me, shattered, scattered, gone. But I will collect the remnants of my soul and try to begin again, my way and with my truth, and this time knowing that what I seek, if there be anything at all, I will never find.

Now I offer some background on how I came to be this lifeless form. First my marriage:

I got involved with my ex husband because he was totally different than what I was used to, I was barely in my twenties yet I needed a change. He was clean cut and stable, or what society describes as ' normal', so I went with it, for a while. I should have known the day I tried to end it that I would never get away. He went to extremes to make me stay and eventually I tired of the game, ended up pregnant and stayed. And thus began my imprisonment. After many moons of fight, strife and struggle I wanted out, badly. I had not enough courage left to actually do it though, for he stripped me of all the courage I once had. So, I locked myself into my visions of love. Not just any love mind you, but the great love.

And then I met "Christopher". Little did I know that this would be the beginning of the end of my life as I knew it. I was drawn to him like a moth to a flame. Never had I experienced such powerful emotions. I was completely out of my mind by the second week of our relationship. I was so captivated by the secrets in his eyes, and I needed to know more. I wanted this feeling of utter enchantment to last forever, no matter the consequence.

I left my husband, I left my house, my belongings, my life. I was under his spell. I existed now within a dream, and my ultimate fantasy had come true. So it seemed that there was indeed a magical currant running through the universe as I had hoped. When someone wishes so hard and for so long, it finally materializes.

He was young, to young I feared, and beautiful, only twenty-two. I blame myself mostly for falling into those mysterious eyes. I created the illusion along with him. I permitted him an outlet for the use of his hypnotic art. Only now can I see that this relationship was based on illusion, magic and fate, and not much more.

Life was his stage, and he charmed everyone within his circle to do his bidding. He was a true Scorpio. It seemed he was always looking for a free ride, for someone else to pick up the tab or make his life easier. The women swooned in his presence and the men were eager to please. Everything had to be his way and the minute I dared to differ I was rudely surprised. He could take any situation and turn it back around to make me look foolish or at fault, and it worked every time. I could never come out the victor, no matter which approach I tried, no matter how trivial the subject. I hadn't realized the war of the minds was a part of love, and so it shouldn't be. I found my self beginning to feel like his mother and his maid, which I found a difficult role to play. I just came out of a very stifling marriage and this was the last thing I wanted to become, for I was tired of obeying and pleasing everyone at my expense, which was the loss of me. Not to mention that he was lazy; he lay on the couch while I went grocery shopping! Now I felt that I just wanted to be left alone, more than I had ever realized. There were strong feelings of independence and steaming anger inside of me, just below the surface and waiting to explode. Yes, it was waiting for the right moment to erupt into the rage that would alter my destiny and ultimately set me free. My anger can rouse the dead if need be, and I began to notice more and more things about him that made me ill at ease. My mind was amiss with confusion. I started to think that I had made a terrible mistake by leaving my home and getting involved with him. I was in control of only half of my soul. He had the other half tightly locked away within the deep darkness of his heart, and I suffered dearly.

Our situation was not only about love, no it was a mystic involvement, something which was beyond our control and there were forces at work which I wasn't even aware of. Strange things would happen when we looked deep within the others eyes. Things I had never seen or felt before. I could see beyond our souls and what I saw I cannot actually in words describe. This was a mystical union and we were *both* in for a big and traumatizing surprise.

As the days passed by I yearned to be free. To be free from anyone's control. And yet I thought to myself, how could this be? I am someone else's prisoner yet again. But this time it was much worse. My husband owned my body but I was in control of my thoughts and my soul. Now those to have been stolen from me. There has to be a way to gain back what I have lost and make myself whole in the process. I want to make the decisions in my life for once, something I have never been able to do as an adult. So I tried to narrow down my choices and plan some affirmative action, I planned a coup. I can't ever go back home again, I know things there will never change and changed I had become. I wanted to take the good that came out of this ordeal and keep it. I earned my freedom and I had managed to finally escape from my husband, as he didn't dare chase after me now.

My thoughts on being alone are mixed. I actually had the most wonderful childhood, however I was a spoiled child I suppose, everyone always took care of everything for me. Not to say it's bad, but now I need to learn to do for myself and at this age and stage, it will not come easy. I need a time of reprogramming my ideals.

The day was not lost completely and I still believed in my magical ability, for now I was getting what I had always wanted - the key to my life. It just came about in ways unexpected. But will I be able to leave Christopher? Do I have the power or the strength to fight him and get back the other part of my soul? And will I die without it - without him and my dream?

Life is about pain, both physical and emotional. I believe the physical ailments heal quicker than the psychological. The body heals itself without further ado, while we are left to our own devices to heal our hearts and souls, provided of course that we have been left with them.

I to am now dying again. Self inflicted suffering, and how I suffer. My judgment has been clouded, I am filled with doubt as to my motives of leaving Christopher. My mind is blank, nothing makes sense, and I feel I am doomed. I knew I would not get away unscathed. He said he would not curse me, but I know he has. He has punished me for leaving and it doesn't matter now, I need him back, at any cost. I cannot live like this. My soul is torn in half, I can't breathe, I can't see anything...but you. Oh, sweet misery you give to me new life all the while killing me. I feel so very alone and I want so badly to cry, but I am afraid to, I know I will never stop again. I can't concentrate on anything, I feel sick. Will I ever get over this? Reality, fantasy, which one is which? Each one offers life and certain death. There is no escaping this, I fear I will never recover. I have been sentenced to a living death.

My quest began with magick, enchantment and the need for

16

change, but what I found was only death. I have always been interested in the beings from the Otherworld, and now I have found out that the angel of death has a name. He is real you see, and he is most commonly known as Azrael. I started off slow and he taught me what he could. Honestly it made me uneasy in the beginning to invoke Death himself. I wasn't actually looking to die and I didn't quite know what to expect. Clearly it's all a matter of mental conditioning, once you lose your initial fear and the concepts that brought about such a state, things begin to change. What was once unknown becomes familiar and welcome. Fear is replaced with love.

And this was beginning of my intensifying relationship with the spirit of Death.

Before I even realized just how obsessed I became with it, I had already begun my journey into the downward spiral of death. Who would have ever imagined that there was so much involved with death? Death is not limited to the physical alone. There are the deaths of many areas of our lives that we must face on a daily basis. I have learned better now how to accept these changes for good and to benefit from them, but when change on the catastrophic level happens it's often very hard to see the good, but it's always there. We just can't see what's happening until the 'smoke clears'.

Within the acceptance of death comes the wisdom of life. We learn and create, for within the black void is the place of creation. Will you go mad in the void or will you create your dreams from it? Without a descent into darkness we would lose the possibility of rebirth -a new life, new ideas, a new direction. Death is letting go and that enables us to embrace the new. Sometimes it's necessary to go into the void to unlock the mysteries of your mind and in the dark silence you shall come to know yourself. Death is all encompassing, it is joy, sorrow, beauty, madness and mystery, but it ultimately changes us for life.

Ah pearls of wisdom, and what I know to be the utter truth, but first I must make it through the dark night of my soul. I have lost faith in everything around me, even with myself. There's nothing left, only death.

I learned about the general nature of Azrael on my own, through rituals, meditations and endless nights spent in graveyards. I searched my soul as I began to know him. I remember one night while I was outside, not thinking about anything in particular, I felt an intense presence behind me. And then I saw him. He did not appear as the skeletal figure I had always envisioned him as, rather he was beautiful. He had thick long black hair and he held a resemblance to all of the other angels of special stature. That is not to say that he hasn't appeared in his other forms as well. Legend has painted him out to be as monstrous as they view death itself. They fear it and so, they assume the messenger and guardian of such a position as his must be as fearful and loathsome. But fear it turns out is the only tormentor here.

Nothing makes sense anymore. The only things I can manage to do are write about my pain and relive my suffering every minute of every day. I have admitted my fault in this situation to Christopher, yet he will not have me. He only torments me further on my daily visits with him. I have been reduced to my most pathetic form. Each day I hope that he will tire and lift the sentence he has placed upon me, but truly, he enjoys seeing me suffer. I may have left him, but as always he has the final say. I remember the day I left all to well. It was one of the most heart-wrenching things I've done. He arrived home and saw me in the driveway, things packed and ready to leave. He dropped to his knees and held me, we were both in near hysterics, but I felt it had to be done. He understood nothing about me.

He has managed to turn this drama around on me. If he loves me so much, as he does proclaim, then why not forgive me my terrible mistake? No, he would much rather spite himself than to ever give in, perhaps due to his young age, lack of life experience and sadistic behavior.

He remains aloof as we sit together and this he sees causes me much grief. He uses me more now as he knows I would do anything for him. I learned that he spent the night with someone else and what little remained of my shattered self completely burned out. It was the ultimate shock, my pain supreme. I felt so sick, the situation was so far out of my control, I thought I would die right there. The universe, it seemed, had played the foulest practical joke on me, my life has gone completely awry. I have no idea what will happen next. Everything is completely out of control. I feel like I am slipping further and further outside the bounds of reality, it scares me to think I might end up insane. I am in a state of complete mental overload, and I cannot bear the pain. I thought I could withstand a fair amount of chaos, but this is to great a force for me to bear. I suppose it's time for me to mold something from this chaos, if I give up to soon I will die or end up crazy. I realize that the best things get their beginnings in a state of chaos, sometimes out of pure necessity. But that will depend if I am able to make it to that point.

Sometimes amidst my insanity the voice of reason sounds aloud. I understand but I am not able to follow through. And that is when I realize that I might not have enough strength left to fight this force. Each day I sink further down into the Underworld, and I really don't mind it. I find my comfort within my insanity now.

~ Many there are that go mad within this black void

For we bring the curse of Darkness

Our gift to the wise ~

Jyade C. −The Legacy

I wrote this poem for him while we were still together. It seemed channeled, the words just poured out, I had no idea it was to all come true, or had perhaps in a previous existence. And now I know it wasn't about him solely, but another.

September, Year One

Memories of Original Sin

My knight of cups, mirror of my soul

Most beloved and gentle spirit

Your eyes take me away

And within the swirling mist a scene unfolds

So hauntingly familiar, yet it remains unknown

A special place, a blessed face

Within the crypt of time

When I look into your eyes I gaze upon your soul

No words are spoken here

For words alone could never tell what is felt beyond the veils of time

Another realm, a meeting place

Where our souls dance as one

Was it some undying oath we made

Seeds sown so long ago that brings you back to me

I become unchained

The ghosts that haunt me slowly fade

I am safe now within your eternal embrace

You evoke the tempest that lives within my ancient blood

What vision is this that now befalls me?

A fierceness unmatched by any other memory

The pain of a seemingly endless separation

And ever came that evil hour when our souls were shattered

The sky turns black, the sea is red

Tidings of woe echo on the wings of an invisible assailant

I will haunt and curse the black and forever starless skies

Until my search for you draws nigh

I am the banshide* which screams and bleeds beyond the twilight gate

All shall hear my song of doom

And now the midnight demon comes

With swiftness I unleashed my rage

Till neither god nor man could rest

Dare I tarry longer in this gloaming void

Love will forever fade away from my unborn human
form

Were we spirits once, my love?

Living beyond the eternal midnight realm

Ripped away and torn in half to now endure love in
this flesh

What's the lesson that we must learn

Our transformation has occurred

A completeness that has now become incomplete

Some day to be restored

Two spirits as one, or one spirit in two

Was it some divine plan to teach us both some vital
lesson

Were we angel, demon or shade

Did we fall and now we feel the pain

Human love and punishment

Both are one, they are the same

No, we were not human once before

I know this when I look into your soul

Jyade Cythrawl

I see us enfolded in the velvet sky

All else is black

Everything but you and I

Where do I end where do you begin

We are the silver circle complete unto itself

And ready to being again

What will be the harvest on this mortal quest

We have been empowered, the time for rest now done

Our chance to be united beyond our sacred veil hangs
upon this human thread

This heresy that's ours to bear

But I see us ever circling skyward

Towards the matrix of our soul

The beauty there awaits us

Beyond the midnight fold

The night brings day

Our time is death

The joy now turns to sorrow

*Banshide; Gaelic for Banshee: woman of the hill, also the
harbinger of death as she wails at the windows and doors of
those about to die

October

Azrael

I am the setting sun

And the dawning of the new day

The lonely in despair will seek me

The rich hide in vain

The children know me not

But still I am the same

I am shrouded in myth and fear

Who would dare to come forth and call my name?

Standing alone in the blackness

Come closer

Step through the mist and gaze upon me

See me for what I am

And what I could be for you

Jyade Cythrawl

I am the ashes and the dust

The rotting and decay beneath the earth

I take what is outworn

And bring it back to being in another form

Kings I have defeated

Their cities lay in waste

I am your shadow, joined as one at birth

I am the calming voice you hear in the velvet darkness

When no one else you hear

There is a comfort within my cold embrace

Come

Look upon me

Touch my darkened face

I watch you from the night side

I am always near

I've come not to destroy

I have not anger

Nor any wrath

My song is sorrow

My voice is rebirth

Trust in me

Fear not

Some will bow with trembling

Others come with arms outstretched

They seek the cold sweetness in the dying breath

If you then have understanding

And dare to call on me

I am known as Death

I am known as Azrael

Chapter 2

(Here starts the break up of the relationship)

November 18

The Promise

We all die a little each day.

Life is about pain, physical or emotional.

The physical probably heals better and faster than the emotional pain.

I to am dying now, again.

Self inflicted suffering. I knew I would get burned, but I did it anyway.

And so my death continues.

This time I become death. Stronger in purpose?

Maybe, but what's the purpose now? I know it not.

A mourning shadow I've become.

And what of the Phoenix in the graveyard on that summer day?

Maybe I'll never know now. It will only serve as a painful memory of what could have been. All was empty, yet full. Full of promise, yet terribly empty - alone.

Never again to see beauty through those eyes.

A lie? A wish? A broken promise?

I am a mourning glory, inflicted with the ultimate pain-

The ultimate sacrifice.

Blood- it's all in the blood.

A part of my soul is lost, my blood runs cold as it falls to the ground.

Pale Shadow, mourning's pride, the blood is gone and now you die.

My beautiful, all is lost.

It never was-

It's illusion, magick.

The spell now done, a wish fulfilled, now its gone.

But it never really existed outside of my own mind.

The day is lost, my life- over.

Sorrow, deep unending sorrow.

I shall shift back into my banshide form and wail continuously at the gates of death.

My raven, my hope - come back to me and let me continue.

I can't win, I can't lose

Life is death and the sky is black

No more moon dancing above me in the land of the dead.

The ice has come and we have failed.

I shall wander through the shadows - forever with the angel of death

I need no other-

Death needs death to grow stronger - survive.

I'm being sucked up into a vortex - never to be released.

White face - black shadow, smell of rotting in the air

Death

Death

He knows my name, now I shall never be the same.

Make the pain into something positive?

Easy to say- no other choice.

Only time will tell.

The end of time..

No light..

It's gone..

Can't say..

Goodbye

ᛗ

Within the Void

A scream

A dream

Within the void you cannot tell

I see my blood wash over this scene

The night sky is black and I feel a foreboding

Amidst the ruins that were my life I hear the
banshides-howling cry

I walk on, I move ahead

To look back now would be my end

In the cold chaotic blackness which now engulfs my
mind

I look to the west

Death is the destroyer of all that is outworn

Jyade Cythrawl

From within its cold embrace I will someday feel the
moonlight against my newborn face

Without the deaths of our past we would be dead
ourselves and trapped

To feel its awesome destruction

you must face the night alone

Be brave

Don't fear

The twilight now does hold you

Heed the call

Find the key

Fulfill your destiny

December 12

Deliver Us from Illusion

A scream in the night

A blinding light

In a flash, all is gone

Dark purple mist moving across time

I felt my destiny

Now I am left asking why

He is slipping now from me

Like sand running through my fingers

I try to close my grip, but still it slips out

Slowly

Slowly

Until all is gone

I fall to the ground

And try to collect it back to me

But it is to late

It has already blended with the earth

I cannot regain what was once mine

All is lost

Forever

Hopelessly

Utterly

Gone

What will become of us?

What could we do?

For us

Against us

I cannot tell

Bitterness

Rage

I become as cold as the tomb

And spit on love

Just as it spits on me

Love is a cruel entity

Sent here only as torture to ones soul

Love is punishment

Ugly

Wicked

It makes you lose your mind

It makes you lose control

It leaves you in utter destruction

Desolation

Unending sorrow

What good is it then to chase this evil entity around?

Love

It would be better to kill than to love

What good is it anyway

Love is evil

Love is decay

Love is of the grave

It leads to death

Love is death

No!

Worse than death

Death is a comfort

Love a tormentor

Love has killed me

Yet I live

But I cannot call this life

Nor is it death

It is nothing

December

Dawn of Insanity

An endless eternity of just passing the time-

Nothing-

Filled with nothing

No focus, can't concentrate

What should I do, I can't go on like this

Coming back, always there

GO!

I *know* what I'm doing

No I don't, do I?

How can I?

Can't eat, can't sleep, feel sick

Coming apart- panic, anxiety

Depression, rage, sorrow

Regret

Cannot function for more than a second at a time

Can't do this- what's going on?

Thought I knew

Had *no* idea

Why must it always rain

Can't think, can't listen, can't smile, can't look

Despair, agony - pain

Ultimate pain - tearing, searing through my soul

Emptiness, dying, but still alive

Never ending pain

Sick, faint, don't know what I am doing

Make it go away!

Every second of every day -

Is you

Is pain

Spirit is broken - torn in half

Dying but no death

When will it stop- never is what I fear

I cannot concentrate

It always rains

Can't think, can't breathe, can't see -

Past you

Pain

Unending pain

Relentless, it won't leave

Insanity - a fine thread now holds me

Such pain - my heart has been ripped out-

And I did it to myself

My heart, my soul, my love

Are lost

Gone

I'm cold, can't feel

Only pain

February. 6

Year Two

The Voice of the North Wind

My breath utters my desire

My desire leads me to death

My life now lies in ruins, forever lost

The hours laugh at me, but it is only time

Time is of no consequence to one already dead

A hand reaches through the darkness, out to me

Come, come and follow me

Hesitantly I run into the blackest night

There is no more guide, there is no light

Only the foreboding in the night

I've lost my way, there is no path

The night is vengeance, I become its wrath

The pain comes from knowing

Now turn your back

You'll never be free

Death is the ecstasy, the final release

I can no longer distinguish pain from pleasure

It's all the same to me

I live for the pleasure in the pain

It is my only relief

I am left waiting

Watching

Sweet pain you give to me new life in my death

All the while killing me

The bird flies on through the rain

It makes no difference

The rain brings life and the bird sees only death

Sitting alone, I look through the world

My mirror is cracked

It distorts all images

I see them all writhe in pain

In their blissful ignorance

I am the woman who peers behind the veil

Speak not a word to me

But listen closely to the cries in the wind

The wind lives, it has a soul

And it carries the voices of long ago

Listen close

What do you hear?

It carries a warning, the warning of life

Do you seek life

Then prepare for your death wise one

There is no life

Only death

Take a bow, release the fight

Now go, run on into the night

The insanity is the plight

Breathe your last, look around

For what you see soon disappears

Leaving you breathless and in despair

Seek thee wise counsel from the ancient sky

Do not hesitate, and never ask why

Things are blurred, time stands still

But just for you, and only once

You were lifted up unto the unknown

Jyade Cythrawl

They gave you a gift

And then plucked out your eyes

Sent back to life, now you see nothing

It makes no sense

But again, what does?

There is no order

Don't ask why

The apparition comes when I look away

It swirls around me

Choking me relentlessly

Cruel memory! Be gone. Leave me!

You've served your purpose

Now leave me to the comforting grave

My torment screams with the banshide

Upon the midnight hill

Always

It will be there

Through out

With out

Time

Be gone from me

I have no name

There is no god

No salvation from my doom

No one to look upon

Now look away

But where do you look?

Into the broken mirror

Nothing to see, the mist covers all

There is no life left in me

The water streaks the surface

Imitating the burning tears that fall across my face

My sweet

The prince of my bitter life

My tears turn to blood as I give you my breath

My desire is free

Free now to haunt others as foolish as me

The strong gales come to carry me

They take my voice

Now I am free

February 7 - New Moon

In the Jaws of Winter

I am surrounded by death

Where's the beauty or the balance

I have not seen the beauty of death since the summer

Now all I have is the pain, grief and sorrow

My death no longer pleases me

I have no release, no escape

I keep dying and I'm tired now

It will not stop

And there's nothing I can do

There is nothing left in me

Winter Darkness

I am nothing

I have nothing

I feel nothing

Only my pain

And my deaths

Many deaths

And still it does not stop

It has left me empty and alone

There is nothing left

Only death

Even in death I have been cheated

Where's the beauty after death

Rebirth

And the balance between life and death

I have all death and sorrow only

My grief is eternal

Never ending

I have been condemned

But by who I cannot tell

Something has found fault with me

Now I am tortured relentlessly

Never ending is my suffering

I don't want to keep dying anymore

The winter has been long and brutal

Will it ever end?

Wait for the spring the Wind said

I cannot make it any longer

My spring for me will never come

I have nothing left to sustain me

All goes dark, now the bird is free

But it's to late, and now death will have me

How I miss the summer

When all was beautiful and alive

The promise has left me

The tree is truly dead

The stones have all been over turned

There is no life left here

No

Only death

I am tired of death

Why won't it leave me?

My life now drags on endlessly

February 7

Shadows in the New Moon

The apple has been poisoned

I no longer want that which was never mine

My honesty is my downfall

I was never one for games

Now will one of you kill me?

Jyade Cythrawl

They all have tried, but none succeeded

They only ripped and stabbed at me

Now they have left me bloody and maimed

How can I live on like this

Now I need one of you to finally murder me

How cruel you all have been

Who will finish it now

It will be easier this time around

I will not fight

I need one more death, my final release

I don't want to live

Will you finish it and kill me?

When the spring comes, please think of me

Now go ahead and kill yourself

But only if you first kill me

You're already dead now in my mind

But your spirit still haunts me

Everything I once loved has been torn away

The new moon is today

But there are no new beginnings for me

Only endings

Many of them

And death

Death is the only thing that has been faithful to me

Now I return the favor to that energy

Death is love

So now I go to him

Love only in death, and so you have won

There is no beauty without pain

And the thorns will rip your flesh

Love is an illusion, this reality I detest

And so you say you love me

Then lay my fears to rest

Give me a rose, and forever look away

I give you the burden of knowing

Knowing what was

And what could have been

Walk around the rest of your life

Wearing my shroud of death

I will watch you from the other side

My grief no longer with me, it becomes your shadow
bride

To remind you always

Of the love

The life

You took from me

Only when we suffer will this wretched spell and the rains
reverse

My wedding gown is tattered, and I'm covered now in
blood

When I loose these shackles

May it be you, my love, that takes my place in hell

February 8

Unnamed

The snow falls fast

A gray and bitter morning

I cry at last

The trees are bare

I know that my spring is nowhere near

With the cold the ice forms around my broken heart

I hear a siren in the distance

It goes to rescue one of the living

How I wish there was someone that could rescue me

All I can do is wait

My life hangs in the balance, hoping for a miracle

But will it ever come?

I shall die waiting, never giving up hope

The hope is what sustains and kills me at the same time

Such foolishness, placing your happiness in the palm of another's hands

Oh but I have and now its to late for me

Does the winter wind blow in the promise of a new start?

Or does it bring with it the end

February 11

The Deceiving Pestilence

It seems as though it never happened.

All is fragmented, not real

Are they memories or is it just a dream?

I cannot tell anymore

Time stands still- or so it seems

But the days do pass, slowly, in my nightmare

Nothing seems to matter and I try to run and hide

But the pain is always there

It only shows up in different forms

I cannot escape it, there's no place left to hide

I would gladly face it but I know that I won't die

This tragedy has become my life

I live to feel the pain

It is my punishment and well deserved

I was the one that took my own life

It was a suicide

But no one knows the penalties until it is to late

Now I must live through my death, no relief in sight

I grow colder in my grave with each day

I pray to end my strife

Pain is my companion, death my only friend

Everything has turned black, I cannot see

But death it seems, will not have me

I've searched him out, but he never came

Take me with you!

Alas, my cries are in vain

Please end my plight, take my pain!

I cannot find my way out of this maze

My mind is tangled, I have gone mad

Jyade Cythrawl

The cruelest of emotions has had its way with me

Do not let love in

Death follows him close behind

Love has no mercy

Death brings release

Love brings only pain

If you're foolish enough to let him in

It will be your ruin

A torturous presence is love- madness at best

It takes your mind

It takes your breath

And then it steals your soul

Love is evil

Love is certain death

Never again will I let love into my miserable life

I shall have my revenge

Love has left me insane

And now I fight for my life

Cruel and wicked is love

Love is worse than death, I will never let it back in

The sun goes black

It always rains

I cannot see

I cannot feel

I do not care

Hear me out in the midnight void!

I listen to the screaming wind

It cries of vengeance

All is black and cold

I curse the world and all of its folly

They should have left me alone

Now I must roam, proclaiming my doom

They will all wish for the day

when they hear of me no more

I will destroy the essence of love wherever I shall find it

Love is the double-edged sword

Bringer of life and death with only one blow

Jyade Cythrawl

Love is to powerful to withstand, it needs to be
destroyed

For he himself is no better than hate

He is a winged destroyer sent from heaven

Love is a deadly plague

Chapter 2

The day of my underworld initiation arrived, my second death. I was to take the plunge totally. I had arrived at the gate of Modgud* without realizing where I was or what I had asked for. I was insane, I was in agony, I was utterly lost. Confusion now reigned. I did not understand what was happening but I saw it all transpiring before me, as if I were viewing a dream.

"Now pay the price, I demand your blood. The ancients have awaited you for some time, now your task begins, and so you shall die. Enter here and now this realm of twilight. Within this exquisite pain you will find new comfort and live within a dream. This beautiful heartache will become your new torture, your inheritance awaits you within the Underworld. This is our legacy; yours, mine and theirs, for this is the land of death. I am your nightmare, your only real friend, and I've hunted you since birth. Now come ancient friend, do not fear but I must tear apart your soul. Close your eyes and let the bleeding begin."

I was out of my mind, I took out a razor and began to cut myself wildly. Blood covered my whole face. I was losing my life, but it was certainly not suicide. Only blood, the price, and so began my Otherworld life. I felt myself fall, down, down, very deep. I knew I had left the boundary of my familiar dimension and I was somewhere very dark. And it was very real you see, for this is a genuine place and now I was an agent of the Otherworld. I saw myself dancing on my own grave, and the blood was everywhere. The whole scene was red and dripping with blood, my blood. I was losing my life, my soul was departing, it was leaving my body.

*Modgud Is the Norse guardian of the Giallar bridge, which is the bridge into the land of the dead. All who pass through must pay her the toll in blood.

Afterwards, I of course amidst my panic and pain, drove to Christopher's. I went over to him, not showing my face which was concealed behind my cape. As I cried he looked behind my veil and saw all the blood. He was shocked, and said he cannot bear to see me in this state. He must have known what was to come for that was our last time together and we had to say goodbye now to each other, forever.

March

The Key

No way in, no way out

Where is the key to unlock this mystery?

I am the key

Where do you look? Now go-

But never leave

Where could I go- where shall I run?

Can't hide from the beginning, won't find the end

Circles, circles - going backward to find the way

Out is through- and still you might never be free

Living in the past found new misery

Thinking it through lead me insane

Backward, forward, round and round

I'm in a maze, no way out, going through the only way

The beginning is the end

The end is the beginning

The circle is both life and death

Release your worry

Lose the fight

only then will you gain insight

Winter

The Warning

Enchanted Lady where have you gone

You've lost sight of the white dove in your search for
Morrigan*

What is this desolate place that you roam

Where is the sun

You've become all shadow

Fading out beyond your twilight world

Have you forgotten all that you've learned?

It seems all you need now is death

And your Underworld

Open your eyes, come out of the dark

Leave the house of death, the banshide will wait

Winter Darkness

The place upon the midnight hill will always be yours

Leave them now or forever be like them

The shadow needs the light as the dawn needs night

The White Lady has come

May you see through her disguise

She's taken you captive

And this her gift, will make you wise

But will you be able to survive?

In time you'll see, In time

The White Lady is the Goddess

And the Banshide

Which screams and bleeds and tears you to pieces

In the silent darkness beyond the night

No longer will you cry for yourself

For you will see their sadness

And a part of it become

As you live with them, and die to the world

You must tell them this

Our legacy of sadness

*Morrigan:

Celtic Goddess

The Morrigan is a triple Goddess. She is the Goddess of war, also known as the Phantom Goddess in triple form and a Goddess of death.

The three that make up The Morrigan are crone Goddesses: Badb- The Fury; Macha – Battle; and Nemain/ Nemon – Venomous (see also Fea- The Hateful One.)

She is associated with the dark moon and crows, for she is a Dark Goddess. Various spellings of her name are, The Morrigu, Morrighan, and Morrigan

.

Dead of Night

Dead of night, where is the light

My mind is slowly draining

The bride wore black and is full of blood

The blood of life which now turns cold

The tempest comes, my race is run

Everything is destroyed in its path

The flowers die, the rivers freeze

Nothings left, only death

Chapter 3

My death continues, but this time I become death. Stronger in purpose? Maybe, to learn. I see now why Death stands alone. He has to, for D/death has no common ground in life. I will remain eternally alone, only me and my death. I cannot bear to interact with others any longer, it becomes a chore, I have nothing in common with them now. So I do what I have to and then I hurry home, and the lonely night welcomes me and I her. And it is within the spirit world that I now reside. It is here that I can only find a comfort, within Deaths cold embrace. He has become my companion, my only friend and together we walk on through the midnight realm. He is my guide, the only light.

August 13,

The Doom of Midnight Hill

Broken glass

Broken dreams

Nothing is ever what it seems

I hear a scream every night

And it wakes me fright

Who is the one that cannot find rest?

I hadn't realized that it was me

The pain of emptiness

You might think it no burden to bear

But it weighs heavily upon my blackened soul

I once flew with the white dove, hope and good fortune

But now I am a banshide, and there is no way out

No release

And so my luck has changed

It brings only disaster

And pain

I hurt all that call upon my name

I cause a terrible sorrow of the spirit

Heartache

Pain

I have brought ruin upon many a soul

And never once on purpose

When I try to love I only maim

My heart is so black I find it hard to breathe

It seems it is to late for me, I must now accept my doom

My fate

There's nothing left for me

Everything is gone

My life is barren

A wasteland of death

The only ones that hear me now are of the midnight realm

But I am stuck you see

I live

Yet I am completely dead

I am not fully free to wander the Underworld

Jyade Cythrawl

And not free to be alive as well

Azrael

Is this your gift to me?

A gift I once gladly accepted

But now I want to live

Maybe you're only protecting me

Because life brings only dread

Why is it that Death himself can make time for me

When no one else I call will come

No soul that still breathes can know my pain

It's to late now

There's nothing left for me to do, but die

Vesper

Vesper

Can you hear them call?

Vesper

Vesper

Now the curtain falls

My blood has changed again

This time it turns to water

There's no life left in me

Maybe now they'll break my chains

And I may freely roam in Hell

Chapter 4

My undead wanderings continue but now begins the realization of my predicament, my true imprisonment within the Underworld and this leads me to a new cycle of events. This is but one part, for there is much, much more to this story. But alas, I can only share what I am able to reveal. The one mentioned in parts of this tale is not Death in the form of Azrael solely, but another that is very dear to me.

I have a special image in the back of my mind, but it is ageless, timeless, not alive. I have arrived at the gate of the North Wind. I quietly look about me and then I proclaim, from the winds of the wings of demons comes now the second of the first; which has already started. I have talked of you and I stand within your power and presence, wherefore may you grant me this last request. Let me descend fully into your realm, see me as a fit extension of yourself. Unveil to me through misery, the power of my living death. And so now he comes. I made a wish so long ago, here where I now stand. I have learned much since that day, now I need the other to find my way. He is a beauty, his hair is black flame. His eyes hold the secrets - the mysteries of time. He is a dark warrior of truth.

Time dances across the Northern sky, like a soldier back from battle I have won. Through out, without, time, I have come. As my feet touch the snow and the wind stings my face I feel for the last time the desolation of this place. Bring new life to the dead. The winter demons come and lead the way into this icy cave and the bird flies in to meet its last fate. On the winds of the wings of demons! Now Come!

And I heard a choir of angels sing to me my doom...

Azazel

Where is my faceless rider?

He who rides the winds of time

Mystic, poet, teacher, sage

I can feel the energy of his arrival as the time draws nigh

He heralds the dawn of a new golden age

And brings with him many of his own race

Beyond the veils of time is where they ride from

Ours is a time when two worlds will collide

I search for the path through time that leads me to your
ageless eyes

Where is my rider of the midnight realm- for I have been
shown the memory of you

Do you still seek me out as well, from beyond the veils
of time

This unseen dimension keeps us apart - maybe until I learn my lessons well

Will you be my guiding light through the darkness of my life

Are you the source of fire that burns within my heart,

That which drives me on in search of answers to this endless fight.

When will you come and speak to me

How can I find you?

I've come so close- where have you gone-

I can't feel you anymore...

Shadow Light

I've traveled through fear and utter darkness

to be with you

And not a word you spoke to me

I am confused

I get deeper within this mystery with each new day

Or am I just insane, it is becoming a fine line

I grow more perplexed

What I thought to be simple is now a true mystery

A puzzle at best and I am missing many pieces even
more so now.

But every day I receive more information

Some things become clear, others more obscure

I thought I was going to figure it all out

But now I am lost within this mystery

You are a mystery

And what is my part in this

I wish I could remember

Perhaps I safe right now within my forgetfulness

What a strange thing this all is

I have crossed the boundary because all of this is for real

A bigger part of me remains in the Otherworld now

I can't explain, but it is true

Can't hide, Shadow Light

*Azazel

Autumn

Death

I am death

Cold

Distant

Calm

I am a corpse still slightly warm

I am death amidst life

Alone

Forlorn

The sweetest melancholy fills my soul, as they seal me in my tomb

The essence of death is what I've become

Void of emotion

Yet I cry out

I stand as a specter among the crowd

Ageless

Timeless

My eyes have seen all

I stand alone, apart from all

Death is my life

My soul

He alone is my comfort

My goal

I have traveled through time to be one with him

To unite with his solemn beauty

And to feel again his somber grace

I have taken human form

But to their realm will I forever belong

Purgatory

I am in love with deaths domain

The underworld

Its solemn beauty is surreal

The peace, time stands still even though I live

In and beyond the gates of the grave is now my home

I have stayed with you even though I was warned to leave

Was I wrong?

*"No, but you will lead another kind of life"

Then in your cold embrace I shall spend an eternal night

In the web of moonlight I catch a glimpse of my former life

It seems so far, so long ago

But now this is what is real

Eros and Thantos

My search has ended

I have found my center

My center is death

Death is my love

Love only in death

Death is love

Death is my brother

My lover

Death is my comfort

My sorrow

I feel now only through him

He keeps me alive, even though I am dead

He lives through me and I him

Together we are life and death

Above and below

The cosmic circle

Reserved for the few

Winter Year Three

A Legacy of Sadness

Azrael! And the legion of my shadowed friends

which reside beyond the obscure mist of time

I summon thy presence here

So that I may seek solace and comfort within your midst

I seek the mysteries that lie within your realm

I have become like you

I am a phantom among the living race

I fear the daylight will no longer recognize my face

I have become a solitary creature

Out of time

Out of place

Although I long for the feeling of another's cold embrace

A living shadow I seek among the ruins of time

A pale complexion, mournings perfection

And his eyes reflect that piercing pain of knowing -

Knowing the sorrow that lies within this place

Winter Darkness

Two can carry the burden more easily than one

My heart is broken, and now encased in ice

We will carry and keep alive the legacy of your forgotten race

The dogs of doom howl on this lonely hill

They cry and sing a beautiful song

But no one else can hear

Their voices cannot penetrate the mortal world

The Wind knows this and swiftly carries their ballad unto me

And I take a sad delight in knowing that I am one of them

Yet I live

And this pain is often to much to bear

Are there any more like me?

Does this sorrowful song reach the ear of any other?

Or am I the only one

I seek deaths poet

A bleeding lover who also dies

And drinks from this pool of death

Only to remain alive

And we shall never breath our last breath

The shadow of life does taunt us

Always there beyond our grasp

But a flower of night will only whither and die

If left to bloom within the light

The fragrance smells the sweetest under the soft
moons glow

The nurturing beam that understands the mysteries

That can only live by lunar light

One can not call the evening primrose evil in its own
right

It is its nature to only bloom at night

And where would the light be without darkness to
compare its beauty to

So you see, there must be a reason for our being

We carry the burdens

Our delight

The extreme sadness of heart

And the mysteries of night

We are the guardians,

The ones who hear your prayers

We can take away your pain

Or awaken you to more

We are the bridge, the balance and the voice

That reaches out through time

In the valley of the shadow

No one ever dies

Gone

But not forgotten

And free to roam the night

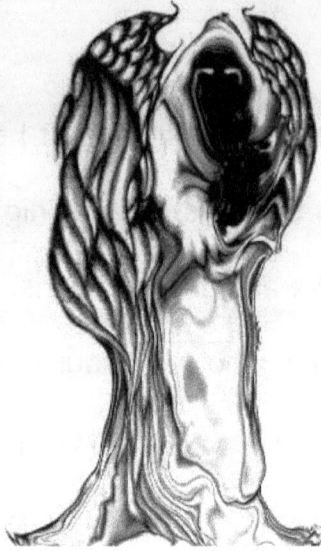

...And so it must be to late for me

For who will love a fallen angel

There's no one now that can save me,

for love itself turns away from me

And the angels do cry, because they once loved me.

Yes you will be sustained,

But even you will never be the same

January 14, Year Four

Ice

There is no life amidst death

A somber shade

I am a specter looking out from beyond the grave

I lookout with wide eyes as I realize my state

Is this is what had to become of me

Death did give a warning, before slamming closed the gate

And now here I must remain

A victim only of life

A fatal encounter that has left me out of breath

Lifeless

Dead

Before life I knew not of death

What is this awful thing that we all dread?

Is it life?

Or death

Jyade Cythrawl

Why are we born?

Why am I here?

Who has played this trick on me

One cannot live if one is never born

Life it seems has scared me more than death

Life has scared me to death

Life is to be feared

It makes less sense than death

My life is a frozen tundra

I am snow-blind

A wasteland has enfolded me

Feeling to much

Now I feel nothing at all

Emotion has robbed me of emotion

Life has killed me

What will death bring?

Maybe a song

Or is oblivion the final resting place

A vast expanse of nothingness

Winter Darkness

From which nothing can escape, and nothing can be born

Life is the reason for it all

Yes, life is to blame, not Death

Life should be the oasis in the middle of all this nothing

A vacation at best

A dream

My dream has become a nightmare

My oasis has become the frozen wasteland

It has all been for naught

Not a single bit of good have I done

Quite the opposite

I've filled my half of the world with night and pain

What a shame

All could have been prevented

Had I not been born

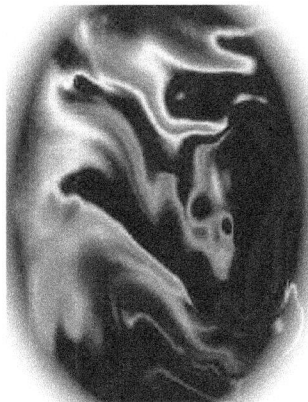

June 11

Path to Sorrow

The memories are faint now

Only shadows dancing across my grave

Barely visible, but I can see them still

How I loved my sweet misery

I want it back

I long for my ghost

My demon lover

I suddenly feel all alone

I have no one to haunt me

No one to die for

No one to kill

*"I can not live without my life

I can not live without my soul"

But where is my life

Who is my soul?

I only love the memory of my murderer now

For *he has found new life

Winter Darkness

As thought did I

But no, there has never been any new life

Only lies

And the clock slowly ticks on...

When will I die?

"Soon, soon

It wont be long now"

The wind cries to me as I quietly pine

Is it spring again? I hadn't even noticed

Do not ask me why

The wind, the banshide and I are all one voice

Hear our wailing cry

In the blackest night on the lonely hill

Across the moors, across all time

In the soul of the land -

We are the soul of the land

Be forewarned

Turn away

If you cross our path

There is no turning back!

You will die

You won't remain as we upon the hill

Your dreams we will take

And there you will lie

We are the sorrow you feel

Forever are we tormented, the sad ones and I

There lies such a power in this state

It has taken on a life of its own

And sealed my fate

Watch the moon rise for the last time

Such a beautiful sight on this desolate night

Here I will wait

Now not able to return to the side of life

All is gray

Can't get through

*from Wuthering Heights; Emily Bronte

* Christopher

Underworld Bliss

Loneliness

My Otherworld reality

No one else here

Only me

Others try but cannot breathe the poison breath

It drives them mad; they go insane and leave again,

For the air that only they can breathe - in the world
which is above

While I am stuck

Alone

No mortals, only me

My Otherness, my Underworld Beings and my Underworld
bliss

For the air down here, no mortals can breath,

It is thick with suffocating Darkness

It drives them mad and rips us apart

Violence

Agony

Sadness

And so they must leave my Underworld bliss

And leave me all alone once more...

Winter Darkness

Whispering winds

Haunting gales

No one sees our light

Mysterious movements

Only moving about at night

See us, join us

And never fear what's right

Your know our voice

You've heard our call

But ignorance is your plight

Hear us

Oh wind of the North!

Take flight

Give us life oh woman who holds the veil

Forsake us not, we who move within the night

Winter, Darkness

Hear us

Help us

Forsake us not

Revive us, remember us

Cold winter night, the awesome North Wind

The wind it comes, it blows again

But will it be for us?

Will it move on

Still searching, will it see us, or hear us yet?

Who will then see us?

And take us for what we really are

Not the light, the plight, the people who remember us
not

No. Tis only night

And memories which lie within the Otherworld

We are nights tears,

We are the night, the legacy of ancient years

Your ancestors and precious ones of olde

Why have we all been forsaken?

Condemned by fools and followers which slumber

Condemning the ancient and sacred beauty of the spirit
world

For there is where we now reside, cast out by mans folly
and pride

Banishment, Ignorance and lies

You and I, we all are one

By shunning us our light has been inverted and now

Illuminates the Underworld

But how many come, how many are chosen

To journey far below the safety of this circus called the
human world

No ear to hear the wind, for foolishness breeds more
fools

Wake now

Winter Darkness

Wake in fright

Did you see, can you feel?

Tis we who roam at night

Ours is the mystery

We make you dream

Your only salvation from the mare, our companion,

Is to eliminate all fear

We can taunt you

But only at night

Without the light

We see

Can you hear?

Wake now

Wake now

Twas only a dream

Jyade Cythrawl

~ We are the night, the legacy of ancient years

Your ancestors and precious ones of olde...

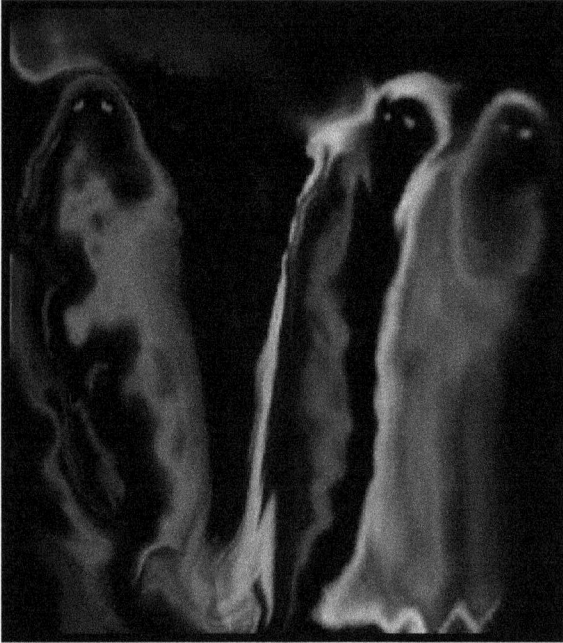

Give us life Oh woman who holds the veil ~

Winter

Hagalaz

Amidst the frost and snow I find new life
The frozen winter has opened up its soul to me
The midnight gale breathes into me the true magic of
this desolate yet beautiful place
The falling snow is life, and my spirit is now at ease
I roam the frozen tundra with renewed awe
The winter demons come, and walk with me
Snow covered moon looks down on the ice of the night
I belong now to the North Wind
am I free now?
Finally free?
A storm approaches.
Ah, tis the furious horde that draws nigh
I take to the sky and join in with them
As do all the chosen dead
My allegiance is to the king

I've been granted rest awhile
I become the voice of enchantment
I've become the voice of the North Wind

Epilogue

As some of you know, this book has been awaiting its release for ages. I wanted to publish this one before I move on to the next batch of manuscripts, in order to form a timeline of sorts. However, I think I've waited far to long.

Also wanted to mention that I have a great family, and they soon realized what a self centered pig headed jerk my ex husband was, I just wanted to clear that up!

This is not a 'fancy' book; the words contained herein are which are of importance, forgive the trivialities which I may have omitted -pictures and such. Now I feel free to move on to the books which were written back in the mid 1990's and beyond! Thanks for your patience!

As always, seek knowledge within the Ancient Darkness,

Jyade

2013

Ancient Legacy Press

"The Voice of the North Wind"

Ancient Legacy Press was created in order to reacquaint others with the angels, ancestors and all the spirits of the Otherworld. My work is dedicated to all of the Watchers and the angels - fallen and otherwise, to make their teachings, true purpose and presence known once again. And to speak of the lore, traditions and the re-enchantment of the Underworld, so that all who listen may again hear the voice of the North Wind; and to Mother Chaos, from which all came and who comes to reclaim her throne in this age of Darkness.

In order to fulfill this mission, it is necessary to dispel the religious & social stigma and hysteria right along side of the centuries of magical ignorance and false information that has accumulated.

For more information please contact us at:

blackmass@aol.com

Ancient Legacy Press

Manchester, New Jersey

USA

www.BlackMagicMarket.com

Facebook:

www.facebook.com/blackmagicmarket
www.facebook.com/jyade.cythrawl

The Original Online Purveys of Darkness Since 1998

ABOUT THE AUTHOR

Jyade Cythrawl is also the author of "The Legacy & The Secret Wisdom of the Black Arts", which attained great success throughout the US and Europe.

The Legacy is about spiritual interaction and attaining wisdom by unconventional means. Jyade Cythrawl is the leading author and expert in her field of 'Spiritual Black Magic', and continues to shed a new perspective on very old subject matter. Jyade has coined the phrase Spiritual Black Magic to differentiate her teachings among the host of other types of black magic.

Her new book, Winter Darkness, deals with the period before hand, her personal battles, love, losses, transformation and interactions with the spirits of the Underworld along her spiritual journey.

She and her readers have come to understand these old phrases, such as black Magic & demonology and surpass and shed new light, meaning and wisdom on these ancient subjects. Jyade's type of black magic is not one of the main stream or of devil worship; it is one of finding wisdom through understanding which leads to enlightenment, and a journey through the Underworld in order to acquire it.

Her first published book, "The Legacy & the Secret Wisdom of the Black Arts", when first released in 2000 sold for $10.95, her choice, in order to make it available to all so that they may be able to receive its teachings.

It is now out of print and has become a collector's item. It is still widely sought after for its contents and popularity. She still sells the few remaining copies on Amazon.

Jyade has been into the Mysteries her whole life, making contact with spiritual beings from a very young age.

Her honesty is reflected through her writing, she hides little, for everyone is on their own journey and can learn from honesty. She concedes that people can't learn what they need to if she will not reveal the things that most would not about themselves.

"It's all about experience, the 'real' world and the spiritual, which co exist", she states, therefore her personal and spiritual life are also revealed through her writings.

Demonic Magic

By

Jyade Cythrawl

ISBN 978-0-9706103-2-4

This is the first modern book of its kind! It was written by a leading demonologist and advocate. This book and its teachings can be applied instantly!

This innovative book talks about demons as teachers and guides, and not something to be feared. You will be taught what demonology and demonic magic really are and how to contact and connect with them!

It teaches the True doctrine of the demons.

This exciting book tells the Truth and goes against what has been written over the past centuries. It also reveals what has been said over the centuries in an easy to understand format.

It expounds in ways that modern practitioners never have, or never dared, and simply because most have had no real experience with these subjects.

This book is in an easy to read and use format. No magickal jargon, no prayers to a Christian god or any magickal hype or preparations!

Some of the topics covered:

Demonology, Demonic Magic, Possession, The Watchers

Demonic Rituals, Book of Demons

Winter Darkness

www.ingramcontent.com/pod-product-compliance
Lightning Source LLC
Chambersburg PA
CBHW031325040426

42443CB00005B/217